Gérard Ausina - Luigi Prodomi

LOURDES

The life of Bernadette - The Apparitions - The Shrines

"The miracle of the candle" (XVIIth Apparition) by Carrier-Belleuse. (Painting from the Hotel Panorama)

ANDRÉ DOUCET PUBLICATION - LOURDES

In the South-West of the Departement of the Hautes-Pyrénées, about 1,200 feet above sea-level, in a beautiful natural setting in the foothills of the Pyrenees, on the banks of the Gave which flows down from Gavarnie, stands Lourdes, the meeting point of the Seven Valleys of the Lavedan.

LOURDES THROUGH HISTORY

In the past, Lourdes was, among all the towns of Bigorre, the one that played the most important part, because of its topographical position and of its great means of defence.

The history of Lourdes is, indeed, closely linked to the history of its castle, which has seen Charlemagne, the black Prince and Duguesclin pass below its walls.

The legend tells us that Charlemagne, on his way back from an expedition in Spain, laid siege to Lourdes, occupied by the Moors, whom he hoped to starve into submission. But the time passed and the citadel remained impregnable. A gigantic eagle one day rose from the azure, flew over the fort end dropped the enormous trout that he was holding in his beak. Mirat, the chief of the Moors, threw the fish down to Charlemagne's soldiers. The Emperor raised the siege, as he thought that the besieged still have plenty of food. Turpin , the bishop of le Puy and a companion of Charlemagne, was granted permission by the Emperor to discuss terms with the besieged. Mirat, confident of Charlemagne's pardon, surrendered. Converted by Turpin, he was christened and took the name of Lorus, which, transmitted to the town, became Lourdes.

And the coat of arms of lourdes has been decorated ever since that time with: "Escutcheon of gules with three towers of gold, built up with sand, upon a rock of silver; above the median tower, a spreadeagle of sand, limbed with gold, holding in his beak a trout of silver; the point, azure, with six mountains of silver - which separate the seven valleys of the Lavedan - watered by a natural Gave".

LOURDES, IN 1858

In 1858, the Castle of Lourdes has lost its former importance. Only the memory of its glorious past remained.

The town had remained a poor small market-town of about 4,000 inhabitants. The small amount of the local trade consisted in supplying provisions to the detachments of troops that were garrisoned there. The locals, mostly farmers, lived peacefully from the hard work in the fields or from the exploitation of stone and slate quarries. In summer the many stage-coaches on their way up to Cauterets or Barèges brought a bit of life to the town, for on the Place du Marcadal was a relay station.

LOURDES, A WORLD FAMOUS PILGRIMAGE CENTRE

Since then, people have coming to Lourdes from all over the world to find out more about the small town, nestling round its parish church at the foot of its castle.

Every year more than 3,500,000 pilgrims, visitors or tourists stop in Lourdes for several days on an organized pilgrimage, for a family stay, or simply to visit the Domain.

Lourdes radiates a special appeal. A unique meeting place, it is for the Christian the revival of his faith, for the invalid a hope for recovery, for the heart a reason to hope.

On the Esplanade the crowd is extremely varied: every continent is represented. But all these nationalities that mix together in Lourdes form a unique community that kneels down before the Crowned Virgin, spreads its arms in the Cross, says its rosary, has a candle burnt, drinks from the taps, follows the Stations of the Cross.

Pilgrims and tourists discover the Grotto of the Apparitions, the Rosary Basilica on which is built the Upper Basilica and the Crypt, and the majestically sober Underground Basilica of St. Pius X, which can hold 20,000 people.

LOURDES, A TOURIST CENTRE

Some people think of Lourdes only as a place of pilgrimage.

It is also one of the best equipped tourist centres. Its many camping sites and 400 hotels have made it the third city in France as far as the hotel business is concerned. It is rich in tourist attractions. You will find perfectly equipped woods and forests, many shady gardens, picnic areas, and open-air swimming-pool, and indoor swimming-pool, a town stadium, a multi-purpose hall for 4,00 people, the Congress hall, the Castle with its Pyrenean Museum, the Museum of Our Lady, the Museum of the "Gemmail", the Grévin Wax Works Museum, the Museum of "Petit Lourdes", the Museum of Lourdes, the Museum of "la Nativité", the Grottos of Saracens, the Pic du Jer funicular railway; two kilometres farther away, the lake (rowing, pike fishing, yachting).

Lourdes, in the heart of the Pyrenees, is also the starting point for guided tours. At the foot of a marvellous mountain range, on the edge of the national Park of the Pyrenees, Lourdes offers a wide range of excursions (coach capacity totalling 5,000 seats) to the impressive sites and the natural curiosities of the area, which are known all over the world: the Cirque of Gavarnie, Pont d'Espagne, Grottes de Bétharram (Bétharram Caves) and of Médous, the Aspin, Aubisque, Tourmalet and Peyresourde passes, the Lac de Gaube and Lac d'Artouste.

In winter, at a short distance from Lourdes, several ski resorts are within easy reach: Barèges, La Mongie, Cauterets, Saint-Lary, Hautacam, Luz-Ardiden, Gavarnie-les-Espécières, Piau-Engaly.

The spiritual vocation of Lourdes is inscribed in the landscape of admirable variety and unique harmony. The remarkable sites and varied curiosities join together to make this little area in the Pyrenees one of the Places in the world where charm and greatness are well worth a second glance. Lourdes cannot be explained; it can only be looked at; that is what we have tried to do.

BERNADETTE SOUBIROUS

Bernadette Soubirous, born in Lourdes on 17th January 1844 in the Boly Mill, was the elder daughter of François Soubirous and Louise Casterot, his wife. She was baptized at St. Pierre's, the parish church, two days later on 9th January, her parents' first wedding anniversary.

Bernadette belonged to a family of millers too trusting and generous to make a decent living from the Boly Mill. The pantries of many families would have remained empty if the Soubirous family had not lent them a few sacks of flour. As is always the case, the number of good customers goes down while the number of those who cannot pay increases. The poor results of the mill led to financial difficulties and the Soubirous family was forced to move several times.

Tribulations did not spare them. When Bernadette was ten months old her mother burnt herself badly and could no longer suckle her child. Marie Laguës, from Bartrès, who had just lost her own child, agreed to be the wet-nurse. Bernadette returned to her parents on 1st april 1848.

Toinette was born two years after Bernadette, then Jean-Marie in 1851 and Justin in 1855.

Times were hard. Louise Soubirous went out cleaning, did laundry and seasonal work to earn a few pence.

During the winter of 1855-56 Bernadette helped her god-mother, Bernarde who ran a Café at the corner of the Rue du Bourg. She did the cleaning and took care of the children. Thus, there was one less hungry mouth to feed at the Soubirous' house.

Bernadette returned to Bartrès in 1857 for the same reason and was employed by her foster mother to watch over the sheeps and also as a servant girl. She came back to Lourdes for good on 21st January 1858. During that period of time, on 27th march 1857, Bernadette's father, François Soubirous was imprisoned for stealing some flour. Maisongrosse, the victim, suspected him because "it was his miserable condition that made me think he was the culprit". He left prison on 4th April 1857, his case being dismissed because of insufficient proof.

In 1858 Bernadette lived with her parents, her sister Toinette, eleven and a half, her brothers Jean-Marie and Justin, respectively six and a half and three years old. They all lived on the ground floor of the Sajous house called the Cachot a wretched cell where criminals used to be imprisoned. At 14 Bernadette was a frail, sickly child. She suffered from asthma and in 1855 had cholera, which stunted her growth. The eldest of four children, she was unable to attend school and was illiterate. She could not go to catechism either and had not as yet made her first communion.

The exceptional destiny of Lourdes, the World famous Pilgrimage Centre, began on 11th February 1858. On Shrove Tuesday at twelve o'clock the Soubirous family had no wood to cook lunch with and Bernadette, with her sister Toinette and Jeanne Abadie went to look for dead wood along the banks of the Gave.

The Cachot

THE FIRST APPARITION: 11th FEBRUARY 1858

"The first time I went to the Grotto was on Thursday, 11th February. I went there with two other girls to gather firewood. When we arrived at the mill, I asked them if they wanted to see the place where the canal flows into the Gave. They said they did. So we walked along the canal and we came to a grotto on the other side. As they wanted to go into the grotto, they had no other choice but to cross the stream. All of a sudden they began to cry. I asked them why. They answered that the water was too cold. So that I could cross without having to take my shoes off, I asked them to help me place some stepping-stones. But they told me that if I wanted to cross, I would have to do like them. I went a bit further along to see if there was a place where i could cross without taking my shoes off. It was no use. So I came back opposite the grotto and began to take off my shoes. I'd just taken off one of my stockings when I heard a noise like a gust of wind.

I turned my head towards the field opposite the grotto and noticed the trees were not swaying. I continued taking off my shoes. I heard the same noise again. As I raised my eyes and looked towards the grotto, I saw a lady in white. She was wearing a white dress, with a white veil, a blue waistband and a yellow rose on each foot, the same colour as the chain of the rosary. I was taken aback. I couldn't believe it. I rubbed my eyes and I looked again and could still see the same lady. I took my rosary from my pocket. I wanted to bless myself but I couldn't raise my hand to my forehead. It fell back down. Then fear took hold of me. My hand was shaking. Yet I remained where I was. The lady took the rosary which was wrapped around her wrist and made the sign of the cross. I tried to do the same and this time managed to. As soon as I had made the sign of the cross my fear disappeared. I knelt down and said my rosary with the beautiful lady. The Vision passed the beads through her hands, but she did not move her lips. After I had finished my rosary she beckoned me to come closer, but I didn't dare to. Then she disappeared suddenly".

Still shaken by the "vision" Bernadette gathered up her pile of wood as best she could and returned home with her sister Antoinette and her friend Jeanne.

Let Bernadette take up the story again. "We went home together. On the way, I asked my companions if they had seen anything. They said they

The Grotto at the time of the Apparitions

hadn't. I asked them the same question again. They said they hadn't seen anything, and added: "Why, did you see something?".

"If you didn't see anything, then I didn't either", I answered.

I thought I'd been mistaken. While we were walking back home my companions kept on asking me what I had seen. I would have preferred not to say anything, but they insisted so much that I made up my mind to tell them. But on one condition: I wanted them to promise that they wouldn't tell anyone else. They promised me that they wouldn't. But hardly had we arrived home than they couldn't contain themselves and blurted our the whole story". Bernadette's parents weren't very pleased. Her mother gave the two sisters a good telling off and a good hiding. She also forbade Bernadette to return to the Grotto of Massabielle.

THE SECOND APPARITION: 14th FEBRUARY 1858

This is how Bernadette described what happened. "I went back to the grotto for the second time the Sunday after. I remember it well because I felt driven by some inner force.

My mother had forbidden me to go back there. After High Mass I went with my sister and my friend to ask my mother again for permission to go to the grotto. She positively refused. She was afraid I'd

The Lacadé Mill (paternal home) as it was at the time of the Apparitions. (Museum of "Petit Lourdes")

fall into the water and miss Vespers. I promised I'd be back by then. So she agreed to let me go. Before leaving I went to the parish church with a flask containing a little holy water that I intended to sprinkle onto the vision at the grotto, if ever I happened to see her again.

When we arrived at the grotto each one of us took her rosary and knelt down to say it.

I had hardly got past the first ten beads when I saw the same lady appear again. I immediately started to sprinkle her with holy water and begged her to say if she came on God's behalf, or else to disappear. I was sprinkling her with water as fast as I could. She was smiling and bowed her head. The more water I sprinkled in her direction the more she smiled and bowed her head.

I noticed she kept on making the same movements, as if to make sure that I understood. Then I took fright and I sprinkled her even faster and kept on doing so until there was no holy water left. When she came to the end of the rosary she vanished".

During that apparition something disquieting occurred. As the two girls who were with Bernadette started to panic, Jeanne Abbadie dislodged a big stone which rolled down near the grotto.

Being deep in ecstasy Bernadette wasn't aware of anything, and when the two girls tried to lift her up in order to lead her away, they couldn't because

The Boly Mill (Bernadette's birth-place) as it was at the time of the Apparitions (Museum of "Petit Lourdes")

she weighed so much. Antoine Nicolau, the sturdy miller, was the one who managed to carry her back to his mill still in deep ecstasy. Needless to say, her mother Louise told her off again, forbade her to return to the grotto, and threatened to punish her if she did.

The Grotto at the time of the Apparitions (Museum of Lourdes)

THE THIRD APPARITION: 18th FEBRUARY 1858

This was one of the four most important Apparitions. For the first time the "lady" spoke. Bernadette takes up the story again. "The third time I went to the grotto was the Thursday after. A few respectable people came with me. They had recommended taking a sheet of paper, a pen and ink, and had advised me to ask the lady to be so kind as to write down anything she had to say. When I begged her to do so, the lady smiled and told me she had so many things to say that it was no use writing it down. She asked me to be so kind as to come every day for two weeks. I agreed to do so. She then added that she didn't promise to make me happy in this world, but in the next. I went back to the grotto every day for two weeks. The vision appeared to me every day, except for one Monday and one Friday".

THE FOURTH APPARITION: 19th FEBRUARY 1858

This was a brief apparition, lasting little more than a quarter of an hour, with no message, completely silent. Bernadette fell into a state of ecstasy after the third Hail Mary. She went pale, her expression changed and turned into a faint smile but betrayed nothing of her inner feelings. One significant detail: for the first time Bernadette had taken with her a blessed candle, which she was to continue to do each time she went back to the grotto, up to March 3rd, the day of the 14th Apparition. Hence the custom in Lourdes of taking candles to light in front of the Grotto.

THE FIFTH APPARITION: 20th FEBRUARY 1858

Some thirty people who had been praying for a quarter of an hour were present when the vision appeared. The ecstatic Bernadette was intently listening. At the end of the apparition great sadness veiled the girl's face. Nobody will ever know anything about what was said. Some say that the Lady taught Bernadette a prayer for herself only.

THE SIXTH APPARITION: 21st FEBRUARY 1858

It was early on a Sunday morning, with one hundred people present. Nothing special happened. The rosary was said and, as usual, Bernadette fell into ecstasy and came to as if after a dream.

For the first time Bernadette was questioned at length by Commissaire Jacomet.

THE SEVENTH APPARITION: 23rd FEBRUARY 1858

On Monday, 22nd February, against her parents' wishes, Bernadette went to the grotto driven by some irresistible force, but there was no apparition that particular day. The girl was disappointed and so were the awaiting crowd. As she returned home, Bernadette wondered wistfully what she could have done which might have displeased the "Lady in white".

On Tuesday, 23rd February, Bernadette got permission from her parents to go down to the grotto, where a crowd of some 100 people were waiting, among them some important members of the community. Her ecstatic state lasted about an hour. Afterwards, the little girl revealed that during this apparition she had been told a secret "for her ears only".

On that 23rd February for the 7th apparition, was also present Doctor Dozous, a scientist and a real disbeliever if ever there was one, who had gone to the grotto to observe Bernadette closely and in the name of science and medicine to thus denounce the "hoax" of Massabielle. Instead of that, what actually happened was the beginning of his conversion. The Doctor's own words are of particular value. "Once in front of the grotto, she (Bernadette) knelt down; took her rosary from her pocket and began to pray. Soon after, her expression visibly changed, a sure sign that she was in contact with the apparition. She followed the "Hail Mary" with her left hand and held a lighted candle in her right. The candle kept being blown out by the gusts of wind from the river. Each time the candle went out, she got the person nearest to her to light it again. I followed her slightest movement closely to see what conclusions could be drawn, and I tried to feel her pulse and check her breathing. In order to do that, I took hold of one of her arms. Her pulse and breathing were perfectly normal. There was no indication whatsoever of the girl being in a state of nervous excitement, which might have affected her organism. When I let go of her arm, she stepped nearer the grotto, and suddenly her face took on a sad expression. Two big tears ran down her cheeks. This sudden change made a lasting impression upon me".

THE EIGHTH APPARITION: 24th FEBRUARY 1858

Penitence!

This was the beginning of the period of penitence. Surrounded by about 300 people Bernadette fell

Bernadette Soubirous - Real life portrait

The Cachot (Museum Grévin of Lourdes)

into ecstasy. Her face betrayed more sadness than joy. She moved forwards on her knees, nodded and shook her head, kissed the ground. The lady's message was of primary importance. "Penitence! Penitence! Penitence! Pray to God on behalf of sinners! Kiss the earth in penitence for sinners!".

The Presbytery (Museum of "Petit Lourdes")

Pyrenean village (Museum of "la Nativité")

THE NINTH APPARITION: 25th FEBRUARY 1858

The miraculous spring

At five o'clock in the morning, despite the rain and cold, 300 people were present for the Apparition. This is what Bernadette said: "One day, she told me to go and drink at the spring. As I couldn't find it, I went to drink at the river. She told me that wasn't where I was supposed to go. And she pointed to the spring for me.

I went there but only found some muddy water. I put my hand in but didn't manage to take any water. I had to scoop the mud away for it was dirty. At the fourth attempt I was able to drink it.

She also asked me to eat some grass near the spring. Then the vision disappeared and I went away".

In the evening of that 25th February Bernadette was questioned by Procureur Impérial Dutour, who threatened to send her to prison unless she promised never to return to the grotto.

THE TENTH APPARITION: 27th FEBRUARY 1858

There had been no apparition on Friday 26th February. This day 600 people were waiting. Bernadette said her rosary, kissed the ground, kept looking at the niche in the grotto, but to no avail.

Bernadette felt upset and worried. On her way back from the grotto, she kept saying: "What can I have possibly done to her? She must be angry with me". Yet, on Saturday 27th February, the apparition was there again. 800 people had come that time. Bernadette fell into silent ecstasy. She was pale, as usual, with sometimes a heavenly smile, sometimes an expression of sadness. The girl drank some water from the spring and performed the usual ritual of penitence.

THE ELEVENTH APPARITION: 28th FEBRUARY 1858

It was a Sunday. The apparition came at about 7 o'clock in the morning. More than 1,000 people were present. Bernadette prayed, kissed the ground, moved forward on her knees as an act of penitence.

Among the crowd stood a high-ranking soldier in uniform, Commandant Renault, who had come from Tarbes to see himself the "extraordinary happenings" in Lourdes. But after High Mass an unpleasant surprise awaited Bernadette. She was taken under guard Procureur Impérial Dutour's office where Juge-Instructeur Ribes was to question her. Although she was threatened with prison, Bernadette answered as always with the same forceful serenity.

THE TWELFTH APPARITION: 1st MARCH 1858

Some fifteen hundred people had come to watch, among whom for the first time was a priest. No message was given that day. However, a curious happening, due to a misunderstanding and popularly called the "Rosary Blessing" gave rise to great enthusiasm.

THE THIRTEENTH APPARITION: 2nd MARCH 1858

Message to the priests!

This date is of prime importance in the history of Lourdes, for the message given to the priests. There was a huge crowd for this apparition. Accompanied by two of her aunts Bernadette went afterwards to see Father Peyramale to inform him of the lady's wishes.

Bernadette said: "She asked me to go and tell the priests to have a chapel built here. I then went to deliver that message to the parish priest. He stared at me for a moment and asked me in a forbidding tone of voice. "What's this lady's name?" I answered that I didn't know. He told me to ask her. The next day I did, but she just kept on smiling. The parish priest told me the lady was making a fool of me and that I'd just as well not go back to the grotto, but I couldn't help it.
Father Peyramale not only wanted to know the lady's name; he also insisted on having the following proof: to see rose-bush down at the grotto bloom in the middle of winter.

THE FOURTEENTH APPARITION: 3rd MARCH 1858

For several hours over 3.000 people had been waiting for Bernadette who arrived at about 7 o'clock. As usual she said the rosary, but the "vision" did not appear. Bernadette went home feeling very sad, while the crowd, disappointed as they were, made disapproving comments because they had waited in vain.
But after school Bernadette felt the "secret invitation" by the lady and, along with one of her uncles, she went back to the grotto and found the lady waiting for her.
"...After saying the rosary", she wrote in her memoirs, "I asked her her name on behalf of Father Peyramale". Her answer was a very sweet smile.
That evening, when the girl told the Father Peyramale about her latest conversation with the "vision", he repeated what he wanted her to do. "If this lady really wants the chapel, let her say her name and make the rose-bush at the grotto bloom".

THE FIFTEENTH APPARITION: 4th MARCH 1858

The long awaited day
For the eagerly awaiting crowd this was to be "the day of the miracle" after two weeks of apparitions, if what the lady had promised was to come true. But it was quite the opposite - just an ordinary apparition like the others, in front of 8,000 people. At the third Hail Mary of the second decade of the rosary, the ecstasy began. Bernadette was now smiling with joy, now looking sad, and this went on for 50 minutes. At eight o'clock she came out of her ecstasy, put out the candle and returned in silence to the Cachot. But there was silence and disappointment also among the crowd, who had been expecting something extraordinary to happen.

In the afternoon Bernadette went to see Father Peyramale to tell him that the lady hadn't given her name, but that she still insisted on the chapel being built. The Priest was adamant: "If the lady wants the chapel she must say her name and also provide the money for it to be built".
There followed a break in the series of Apparitions. For 20 days Bernadette didn't go down to the grotto. She no longer felt irresistibly drawn. Life went on at its tranquil pace as before. Bernadette attended school more regularly, yet she couldn't get out of her mind the exceptional experience she had been through and she still didn't know who that lady was.

THE SIXTEENTH APPARITION: 25th MARCH 1858
The long awaited name.
Thursday 25th March, the Annunciation, is the most important date in the history of Lourdes. At last, the "vision" revealed her name.
Bernadette tells the story quite simply: "I asked her 3 times who she was. She just kept smiling. I tentatively asked her once again. This time she raised her eyes to Heaven, brought her hands together as to pray and said "I am the Immaculate Conception".

The Apparition (Museum Grévin of Lourdes)

Those were her last words to me. Her eyes were blue. Over two weeks she confided three secrets to me which I was not to reveal to anyone. Until this day I have kept my promise".

Bernadette continued her story as follows: "So I went back to see Father Peyramale and tell him that the lady had said she was the Immaculate Conception. He asked me if I was sure. I answered that I was and added that, so as not to forget the words, I had kept saying them to myself all the way back".

Father Peyramale, deeply disturbed by the "vision's" answer, wrote at once to the Bishop of Tarbes to inform him about it. Bernadette's simplicity and humility had from now on convinced him that she was telling the truth.

One detail had especially struck him. Bernadette didn't understand the words she had repeated: "I am the Immaculate Conception".

Only the Virgin Mary herself could have said them. That was sufficient reason to believe the girl, even if the rose-bush hadn't bloomed, as he had asked. Father Peyramale was to say later: "The rose-bush didn't bloom, but water did indeed spring forth".

THE SEVENTEENTH APPARITION: 7th APRIL 1858

The miracle of the candle

This apparition had a very special witness: Doctor Dozous, the disbelieving scientist who had also been present for the 7th apparition. He was lucky enough to witness the miracle of the candle; or perhaps we should say he received God's grace. During her state of ecstasy Bernadette was holding a big candle in her right hand with her left hand cupped round the flame. All the crowd were awestruck to see the flame lick her fingers without leaving any burns. Doctor Dozous observed the incident and timed it. The phenomenon lasted a good quarter of an hour.

When Bernadette had come out of her state of ecstasy, Doctor Dozous examined her hand. There was no trace of burns. He then put the flame near Bernadette's hands, but the girl cried: "Stop, you're burning me!". The Doctor couldn't get over it. He openly declared: "Now I believe it. I've seen it with my own eyes!".

THE EIGHTEENTH APPARITION: 16th JULY 1858

Never more beautiful

On 3rd June, when she was fourteen and a half, Bernadette made her First Communion, thus realizing her wish to receive Jesus.

She had been longing for this day and she had put into its preparation so much dedicated effort by conscientiously studying the catechism.

Father Peyramale himself was impressed by the girl's eagerness and seriousness. "She has been transformed in such a miraculous way", he wrote to the Bishop of Tarbes.

On 16th July, the Feast of Our Lady of Mount Carmel, Bernadette again felt mysteriously drawn to the grotto. She didn't know what to do, for access to the grotto was barred. Her Aunt Lucie found a solution - to go there by another path. So, at sunset, in the company of her Aunt Lucy and two other people, Bernadette went along the right bank of the Gave and stopped about 150 yards from the fenced-off grotto. This was to be her last encounter with the "lady".

The "lady" appeared as soon as Bernadette started saying the rosary. Her state of ecstasy lasted a quarter of an hour, during which time the "lady in white" said farewell to Bernadette.

"How did you manage to see her from such a distance and with the barrier in front of the grotto?" her friends asked.

"I had the impression of being right in front of the grotto, just as near as I was the other times. I saw only the Virgin. She was more beautiful than ever!".

Bernadette goes to the parish priest to tell him of the wish communicated by the Apparition (Museum Grévin of Lourdes)

QUE SOY
ERA
IMMACULADA COUNCEPCIOU

Boly Mill - the house where Bernadette was born

THE BOLY MILL

The Soubirous family lived in the Boly Mill when Bernadette was born on 7th January 1844. Her parents, poor millers, were generally known in Lourdes as the "Millers of Boly".

Bernadette left this house when she was but a few months old, when her mother, who was expecting another child, received severe burns when she fell in the fire. The child was therefore sent to Marie Laguës (née Aravant) to be nursed the 11th April 1846.

Before the French Revolution it belonged to Anna de Candebotte who married an English doctor, David Boly, who gave his name to the mill. The Soubirous family came to live there from 9th January 1843 till 24th June 1854.

Bernadette was born there on 7th January 1844. On the ground floor you can read about the history of the mill since its creation and see how it worked. On the first floor, the room where Bernadette was born.

Boly Mill - The room where Bernadette was born

FAMILLE SOUBIROUS

*Soubirous's family.
At the center of the photo:
Bernadette with the white
"capulet".*

15

THE CACHOT

This humble dwelling in the Rue des Petits-Fossés has been called the Cachot because it was used as a jail. The only room, 4.4 metres by 4 metres, accommodated the six members of the Soubirous family: the father, the mother, Bernadette, Toinette, Jean-Marie and little Justin.

It is from the Cachot that Bernadette went on 11th February 1858 to fetch some firewood at Massabielle.

On 21st January 1858 she came back to the poverty of the "cachot". From 11th February to 16th July 1858 she saw the Holy Virgin 18 times. On 15th July 1860 she was taken into the hospice in Lourdes, run by the Sisters of Nevers. On 4th July 1866 she left the hospice to enter the congregation of the Sisters of Nevers as a novice. After taking the veil on 30th October 1867, she was to stay for about 12 years in the convent, still plagued with bouts of asthma. It was asthma which finally caused her death on 16th April 1879, at the age of 35.

The Virgin of Good Welcome

BERNADETTE
à prié devant cette statue
placée dans l'église paroissiale.

The Lourdes Hospice

Bernadette in her shrine in Nevers

Maison Paternelle (Bernadette's father's house)

THE MAISON PATERNELLE

As you go up the street you will see it on the left. Its real name is the Lacadé mill. It is similar to the Boly mill and belonged at the time of the Apparitions to Monsieur Lacadé, the Mayor of Lourdes. In July 1863 Father Peyramale rented it for the Soubirous family. Then in 1867 the Bishop of Tarbes gave it to Bernadette's father at that time Bernadette was a boarder at the hospice so that she could get some schooling, and she often came to sleep at her parents: Just inside the house on the right you can see the machinery of the mill and opposite the kitchen in which Bernadette bid farewell to her family. Going up the wooden staircase you reach the bedroom where souvenirs of Bernadette and her family are on show. Her mother died there on 8th December 1866, her father in 1871.

FRANÇOIS SOUBIROUS

Bernadette's father, born in Lourdes on 7th July 1807, he married Louise Casterot on 9th January 1843. He died on 4th March 1871. He was to remain a poor miller all his life. On 24th June 1854 he and his family were forced to move out of the Boly Mill and go to the "cachot".

LOUISE CASTEROT

Bernadette's mother, born in Lourdes on 28th September 1825, she had 9 children of whom 5 survived: Bernadette, Antoinette, Jean-Marie, Justin and Pierre. She gave her children a strict upbringing. At first she didn't believe in the apparitions, but later often accompanied her daughter to the Grotto. She died on 8th December 1866.

François Soubirous - Portrait on show in the Maison Paternelle

Louise Casterot - Portrait on show at the Maison Paternelle

Bernadette's bedroom

Bernadette's parents bedroom

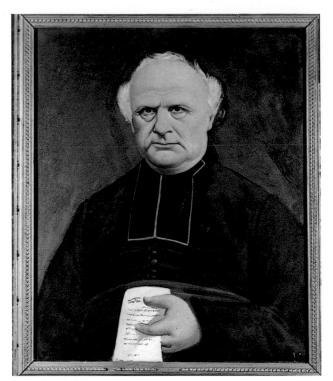

Father Peyramale

The font in which Bernadette was baptised on 9th January 1844

FATHER PEYRAMALE

He was born in 1811. After being the almoner at the civil and military hospital in Tarbes he became in 1854 the Curé Doyen de Lourdes (the Dean) at the age of 43. He was remarkable for his caution and it wasn't until Saint Bernadette had revealed to him that the Lady was "the Immaculate Conception" that he worked with all his zeal for the service of Our Lady of Lourdes.

Parish church

BARTRÈS

A small village, 3 kilometers from Lourdes, where, in 1844, Bernadette was sent to be nursed at the Laguës'. They were kind farners who had just lost a son in his early childhood. Bernadette took the place of the missing son. Marie Laguës (née Aravant) not only fed Bernadette, but she gave her motherly love which never died.

Bartrès - The Laguës house - The kitchen

Bartrès - The sheep fold

THE SANCTUARIES

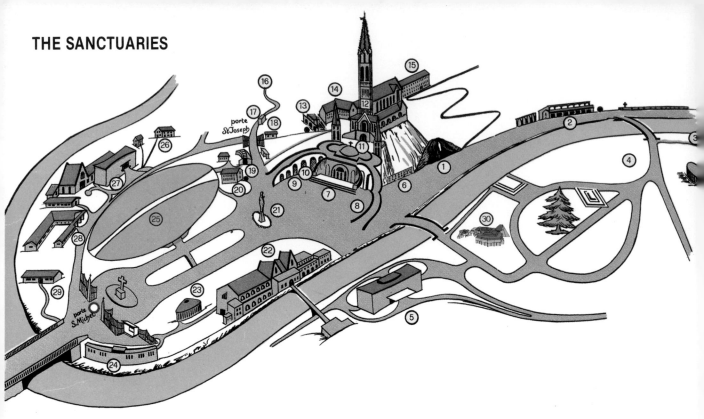

1 - Grotto
2 - Baths
3 - Stations of the Cross for the sick
4 - Prairie - Meeting point for the young
5 - New centre for the sick Accueil Notre-Dame transit room
6 - Drinking taps
7 - Rosary Basilica
8 - Tourists and people on their own. One-day pilgrims Medical bureau (photos of miraculous cures)
   'Porte ouverte'
   Hospitalité
   Pastorale familiale
9 - For young people
10 - St Bernadette's altar
11 - Crypt
12 - Upper Basilica (Immaculate Conception)
13 - Stations of the Cross
14 - Chapel of Reconciliations (Confessions)
   Room Mgr Laurence
   Bureaux (for sending water from the Grotto)
15 - Chaplains' residence
16 - Road to the City of the Poor and youth camp

17 - Bernadette cinema and slide show
18 - Office of Secours catholique
19 - Pilgrimage office
   Lost property office
   Service d'entraide
   Printers
20 - Conference rooms - Forum
   Abri des pèlerins (shelter)
21 - Crowned Virgin
22 - Accueil Notre Dame transit room
23 - St Joseph's church
24 - Abri St Michel
25 - Underground Basilica (St Pius X)
26 - Légion de Marie
27 - Pavillon Notre-Dame
   Mementoes of Bernadette
   Gemmail (glass work) - Sacred art
   Salle Notre-Dame - Information Eucharistic
   Union Pax Christi
   Over 65's - Hospitalité
28 - Pavillon missionaire (missionary exhibition)
29 - Pavillon du lac (A.C.)
30 - Church St Bernadette

The Esplanade of the Sanctuaries, bordered by two ramps that extended for 130 metres, gives access to the Rosary Basilica. Its gigantic dome is level with the Crypt, a chapel built on the very rock of the Grotto. This chapel forms the pedestal of the Upper Basilica, which towers over the Domain. The classical style of the three superimposed churches is in striking contrast to the imposing underground Basilica of Pius X, built entirely of reinforced concrete.

Below, in front of the Gave, is the miraculous Grotto, where the Apparitions took place. On the left, behind the altar, is the Spring which supplies the taps and the Baths.

On the right side of the Grotto a twisting path leads to the fourteen Stations of the Cross.

THE MEANING OF THE WORD BASILICA

The three main churches in the Domain have been honoured by the name of BASILICA, for they have received the special favours of several Popes. As a sign of their approval of their existence, portraits can be seen in mosaic of Pope Pius X and Pius IX on the facade of the Upper Basilica and of the Crypt and of Leo XIII and of Pius XII on either side of the entrance to the Rosary Basilica.

THE UPPER BASILICA

The Upper Basilica, called the Immaculate Conception, was designed by the architect Hippolyte Durand. It is composed of one single nave, divided into five equal bays. In 1908, it was framed by two bell-turrets which link it to the Rosary Basilica. Begun in 1862, it was opened for public worship on 15th August 1871, and consecrated on 2nd July 1876 by Cardinal Guibert, the Archbishop of Paris. Built with stone from Lourdes, its Gothic style spire rises 70 metres from the ground.

Inside, the columns and arcades are made of stone from Angoulême, whereas the High altar is made of Carrara Marble, with the statue of Our lady of Lourdes, by Cabuchet, standing above.

Twenty-one altars adorn the Basilica, which can seat 1,000 people. The organ, made of Russian oak, is composed of 25 organ-stops. It was inaugurated in 1873.

◀ *Interior of the Basilica*

THE CRYPT

The Crypt, situated between the Upper Basilica and the Rosary Basilica, stands on the Rock of Massabielle.

It was built in 1863-66.

Bernadette, just before going to the Convent in Nevers, attended its consecration on 9th May 1866. It is composed of 3 naves with ribbed vaults, and the whole structure is supported by 28 marble columns. The high altar dedicated to the Virgin Mary was renovated in 1966 and 1973. Above, is a Virgin and Child sculpted by Joseph FABISCH in 1868.

Hewn out of the rock, the Crypt is surprisingly small, which helps to reinforce its stability. Its architect was called Hyppolyte Duran. In 1904 you could only enter the Crypt through the galleries on either side, very narrow (3m 20 = 10ft) and entirely covered with ex votos.

Now you can enter directly by the wide central alley hewn out of the rock. It wasn't until 1972 that the alley and galleries formed a whole, reserved for the celebration of Low Mass.

The Crypt

Mass in front of the Rosary Basilica

The Virgin of the Rosary and St. Dominic

Inside of the Rosary Basilica

THE ROSARY BASILICA

It received the title of Lower Basilica in 1929. It was begun in 1883 by the architect Hardi and finished in 1889. It was consacrated in 1901.

Only the Rosary Basilica has no entrance for the handicapped. Note that it was realized 30 years after the Apparitions. Above the entrance is a bas relief representing the Virgin holding the child Jesus who is giving a rosary to Saint Dominic. On the left is St Bernadette's chapel between the chapels of Pascal Baylon and of Notre-Dame de Guadaloupe. Inside, the great central dome which is 22 metres high is decorated with a mosaic of Our Lady of Lourdes (a work of the painter Edgar Maxence 1920). The Basilica measures 52 metres by 48 metres and can hold 2500 people. The inside structure is in the form of a Greek cross but its style is Romano-Byzantine. (It can seat 1500 peo-

ple). The three naves are each 14 metres wide. The golden Virgin of Our Lady of Lourdes, dominating the altar, was realized by the goldsmith Armand Caillat from Lyons in 1897. The 15 chapels with their 15 mosaics which surround the central nave are dedicated to the 15 mysteries of the Rosary. (See description and details of these mosaics on the following pages). They are the work of Facchina de Paris after designs by various artists (1895 to 1907).

The windows in the dome, those in the apse, and the glasswork in the central door are by the artist in stained glass Claudius Lavergne. The organ by Cavaillé-Coll (1897), restored in 1972, has 52 stops and a portable electronic keyboard. Note that the Blessing of the Sick takes place in the afternoon on the square in front of the Rosary Basilica.

2nd Glorius Mystery: the Ascension

3rd Glorius Mystery: the descent of the Holy Ghost

4th Glorius Mystery: the Assumption of Mary into Heaven

5th Glorius Mystery: Coronation of Mary in Heaven

29

2nd Joyful Mystery: the Visitation

3rd Joyful Mystery: the birth of Jesus

4th Joyful Mystery: Jesus presented in the Temple

5th Joyful Mystery: Jesus refound in the Temple

5th Sorrowful Mystery: the Crucifixion

1st Sorrowful Mystery: the agony of Jesus in the garden of Olives

2nd Sorrowful Mystery: the Flagellation

3rd Sorrowful Mystery: the Crowning with thorns

4th Sorrowful Mystery: the Ascent to Calvary

THE BASILICA OF SAINT PIUS X

This underground Basilica has a surface area of 1200 sq metres. As you leave the Rosary Basilica, you will see it on your right and one of its six entrances is just to the right of the Crowned Virgin. It has six entrances which easily allow the coming and going of pilgrims on foot as well as those in invalid carriages.

It was consecrated on 25th March 1958, feast of the Annunciation and Centenary of the Apparitions, by Cardinal Roncalli who was to become Pope John XXIII.

The architects were Pierre Pinsard, André Le Donne and Pierre Vago. 201 metres long and 81 metres wide the Underground Basilica can hold 27000 people. In the centre is the high altar for concelebrations.

During the pilgrimage season there is every Sunday and Wednesday an international mass. More than just a formal liturgy, it is the expression of the universal nature of Faith in Lourdes. The Blessed Sacrament Procession, which usually takes place on the Esplanade, is held here in rainy weather.

Notice the magnificent works of glass: Notre Dame des lumières by Tony Agostini (near the East vestry). And also the rowing-boat of Pierre de Meb for the first pilgrimage of the mentally handicapped, and of course, the 15 Stations of the Cross (in spun glass), by the painter Denys de Solère (1979).

The Underground Basilica of St. Pius X

Church St. Bernadette

1988 · THE SAINT BERNADETTE CHURCH

The new Saint Bernadette church can hold 5,000 people and also includes several convention rooms which can receive 50 to 400 people.

Inside, the church can be divided into two by a partition. It measures 100x80 metres. It took 17 months to build it. It was designed by Jean-Paul Félix, Cyril Despre, Jean-Paul Guinard and Dominique Yvon.

It is a very modern work, spacious and particularly bright, its large windows allow daylight to enter freely.

It was consecrated on 25th March, the Feast of the Annunciation, by Monsignor Donze.

It was his last blessing given as Bishop of tarbes and Lourdes for, after this moving ceremony, Monsignor Donze handed over his duties to Monsignor Sahuquet who thus became the new Bishop of Tarbes and Lourdes.

34

Interior of the Church St. Bernadette

THE BRETON CALVARY ▶

Going on towards St Michael's gate you will see the Breton Calvary. It is 12 metres high and the statue of Christ 2 metres high. The other statues represent Our Lady, St John the Evangelist Saint Longin and Saint Mary Magdelen. It was sculpted by Hermot de Lannion in 1900 and is a gift from the dioceses of Rennes, Quimper, Vannes and Saint Brieuc.

1995 - ADORATION CHAPEL

Situated to the left of St. Bernadette's Church, the Adoration Chapel is a haven of Peace and simplicity conducive to Prayer and Meditation.
A central column housing the Blessed Sacrament recalls the "Pillar of Fire" which led the People of God across the desert to the Promised Land.
From April to September: 8.45 am to 4 pm: The chapel was blessed on the 18th June 1995.

THE DRINKING TAPS AND THE SPRING

"Go and drink at the spring and wash yourself there"
(Apparition Thursday 25th February 1858)

The spring which emerged when Bernadette dug the earth following the Virgin's instructions, now flows at the rate of 122,400 litres a day (85 litres per minute or 5,000 litres per hour).
This water feeds the taps (on the left of the Grotto) and a reservoir (called the Rosary) of 450,000 litres, built under the northern part of the Rosary Basilica, enables an increase in the flow of water on particularly busy days, such as 15th August (when there are about 50,000 people).

The drinking taps

THE BATHS

When you are facing the Grotto, the baths are several yards to your right. They are made of stone and are 16 in number. They were constructed in 1955. Hundreds of able-bodied or sick people bathe there every day helped by qualified volunteers. The water is changed twice every 24 hours.

They are open all year:
weekdays from 9am to 11am and from 2pm to 4pm.
Sundays and Feast days from 2pm to 4pm.
The words of the Virgin: "Go and drink at the spring and wash yourself there". Here we can cleanse our body and wash away our sins.

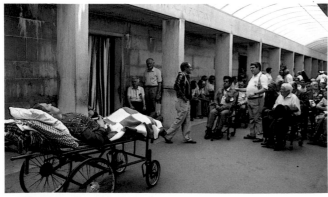

The baths

Inside the baths

THE GROTTO OF MASSABIELLE

Here the Virgin appeared to Bernadette 18 times. The name of Massabielle comes from "Massevielle" which, in Bigourdan, means "old rock". It is a mass of rock about 27 metres (= 85 ft) high covered in ivy and is blackened by the smoke from the candles which burn day and night.

The inside is formed by three adjoining openings: the biggest is 8 metres deep (25 ft), 5 metres wide (15 ft) and 6 metres hight (18 ft).

Above and to the right is an oval-shaped recess where the Immaculate appeared to Bernadette and where, on 4th March 1864, was placed and blessed a statue in white Carare marble, a work by the sculptor Fabish de Léon. On its pedestal is engraved in the local dialect (bigourdan) "QUE SOY ERA IMMACULADA CONCEPCIOU" ("I am the Immaculate Conception"). Those were the words said by the Virgin to Bernadette during the 18th apparition on 25th March 1858. In front of this grotto ran a stream of water from the Savy mill. The Grotto as we know it today was finished in 1955. After being cleaned inside and lowered a few metres it has been covered with slabs of marble. In the centre an altar has been built. In front of the Grotto is a huge candelabrum on which candles burn unceasingly, a symbol of the devotion of pilgrims who come to Lourdes.

Inside the Grotto on the left is the spring which flows from the rock. It is covered by a transparent plaque of glass and is illuminated. Every day during the pilgrimage season, from 6am to 9.30pm, every hour, masses are celebrated in various languages.

POPE'S VISIT ON THE 14th AND 15th OF AUGUST 2004

The Highlights of this event:

The Pope landed at Lourdes Airport on the 14th of August on a brilliant sunny day.
After the official reception, he arrived at the Grotto at midday in order to meditate a while alone and to drink the Water from the Spring.
In the afternoon, the Rosary procession took place; it went from the Grotto to the square in front of the Basilica where the five Luminous Mysteries were recited.
The Pope came as a Pilgrim and as a sick person. In front of the crowd acclaiming him, he raised his rosary high in the air in order to remind us that, above all things, we had come to Lourdes to unite ourselves in prayer with him.
The candlelight procession, that evening, began with the Pope's blessing of the pilgrims from the balcony of the hospital "Our Lady".
On the 15th of August the celebrations began under a burning sun with the Assumption mass in the immense meadow where 200,000 Pilgrims awaited the Pope to commune with him.
His departure and moving farewell at the Grotto, which took place in an unbelievable reverential silence, ended this memorable day of the 15th august 2004.

Photo Viron

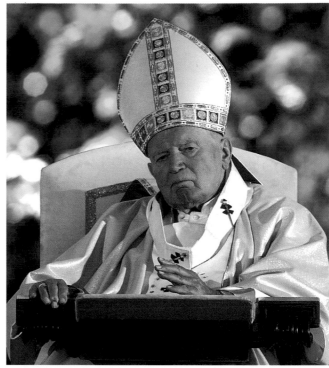

The new "ACCUEIL NOTRE-DAME". This five-storey building was opened o 7th April 1997. It has a capacity of 904 beds and full modern hospital facilities for the benefit of sick pilgrims who come to Lourdes.
Architects: A. and S. Gresy - Photo: M. Durand - O. Vaudoit

Accueil Notre-Dame

The great Esplanade at Lourdes whose centre is dominated by the statue of Our Lady Crowned. It dates from 1877 and is the work of the sculptor Raffl. The original model is on display in the "Bernadette Museum" in Lourdes.

THE PROCESSIONS IN LOURDES

There are two daily processions at the grotto from Easter to October: the Blessed Sacrament and the Torchlight Processions.

The Blessed Sacrament Procession leaves from the Grotto at 4.30 p.m. and slowly wends its way along the Esplanade to finish in front of the Rosary Basilica for the Benediction. The first Blessed Sacrament Procession took place on the 27th of August 1887. The Torchlight procession begins at the Grotto at 8.45 p.m. with the singing of the "Salve Regina", the saying of the Rosary and the singing of the Ave Maria.

Our Lady asked Bernadette for processions. It is the Pilgrims' way, in unity to God and to our salvation.

◀ *Torchlight procession*

As you walk back to the square in front of the Rosary Basilica, we would like to explain what the Rosary Pilgrimage represents for Lourdes. It always takes place at the beginning of October and the French Rosary Pilgrimage has existed since 1908.

Father Rivals (inspired by Father Luquet) accepted the idea and sought the blessing of Pope Pius X. On 17th October 1908 a special train left Toulouse with 700 pilgrims on board. So the idea was first launched in Toulouse by the director of the Rosary, Father Rivals, and the whole of France followed his impetus in 1911. The Rosary Pilgrimage became a national one in 1923.

Rosary Pilgrimage, mass and blessing of the sick

THE STATIONS OF THE CROSS

On the crest of the Espelugues, above the Domain, a monumental Stations of the Cross was erected. In 1885, a cross brought from Jerusalem had been put up there.

The fourteen Stations by Raffl, consist of colossal groups, whose statues in cast-iron are 2 metres high. The first station was consecrated on 5th October 1901 and were inaugurated on September 14th 1912.

4th Station: Jesus meets His Holy Mother

1st Station: jesus is condemned to death

2nd Station: Jesus is given His cross to bear

3rd Station: Jesus falls for the first time

5th Station: Simon helps Jesus to carry the His Cross

6th Station: A Pious woman wipes Jesus' face

7th Station: Jesus falls for the second time

8th Station: Jesus conforts the young women of Jerusalem

9th Station: Jesus falls for the third time

11th Station: Jesus is nailed to the Cross

10th Station: Jesus is stripped of His garments

12th Station: The death of Our Lord (detail)

12th Station: The death of Our Lord ▶

54

1 - 13th Station: Jesus is taken down from the Cross
2 - 13th Station: detail
3 - 14th Station: The shrouding in the Sepulchre
4 - 15th Station: The Resurrection
5 - 14th Station: detail

The castle

THE CASTLE

The fortified Castle of Lourdes, on its rocky peak, towers above the valley of the Gave and the Domain to the West, and above the Upper-town to the East.

From the top of the keep the visitor has a panoramic view over the valley and the mountains that surround Lourdes.

Because of its strategic location Lourdes played a prominent role in the past. A first-rate military post, it held off many attacks. It became a state prison at the end of the XVIIth century.

Today it houses the Pyrenean Museum and displays a selection of the popular crafts and traditions of the Pyrenees.

Pyrenaen museum

The Lourdes Town-hall

An example of the "Gemmail" art

The 4,000 seat multi-purpose hall

The Congress Hall

The lake of Lourdes

The golf court of Lourdes

THE LAKE OF LOURDES

The Lake of Lourdes is 3 km from the town-centre. Leave Lourdes on the road to Pau par Soumoulou, and after the stadium on your way out of the town, turn left into the "quartier Biscaye". Follow the road to a sharp turning on the left and this will bring you directly to the landing-stage. In this magnificent setting, you can hire a rowing-boat, a pedalo (pedal boat), fish or simply have a drink or a bite to eat at the café and make the most of the calm and beauty of the surroundings.

If you enjoy walking, you can go round the lake on foot. Turn right just after the car-park and you'll go through the magnificent Lourdes **golf-course** (18 holes), built in 1988-89.

The Pic du Jer cable-car

THE PIC DU JER

Le petit Jer (altitude 709 m) - Le grand Jer (altitude 948 m)

Still on the national 21, direction Argelès, further along from the Béout cable-car on the left in a bend you'll find the departure point for the pic du Jer. Go up by the funicular railway or go round the building and follow the path marked out by the Tourist Office. Once you've reached the pass (668 m) you can get to the petit Jer and its three crosses which overlook the town or you can go to the grand Jer (observatory). Magnificent view of Lourdes. Worth pointing out too are the Grottes des Sarrazins. Direction Argelès, turn right just before the level crossing and right again at the lights into the avenue Roger Cazenave. 30 minute guided visit underneath the town.

LOURDES, A BASE FOR EXCURSIONS IN THE PYRENEES

Lourdes, in the heart of the Pyrenees, is the starting point for guided tours, the real centre of Pyrenean tourism. At the door of a very wide geographical area, at the foot of a marvellous mountain range, at the border of the National Park, Lourdes offers its visitors a wide range of excursions, natural curiosities, attractions of great richness and surprising variety.

Majestic views and outings for tourists:

Cirque de Gavarnie, Pont d'Espagne, Grottes de Bétharram, Grottes de Médous, Cols d'Aspin, d'Aubisque, du Tourmalet, de Peyresourde, the Lakes of Gaube, of d'Artouste, and many more places worth visiting.

Spas:

Argelès-Gazost, Bagnères-de-Bigorre, Barèges, Beaucens, Capvern-les-Bains, Cauterets, Loures-Barbazan, Luz-Saint-Sauveur.

Nine ski-resorts within a radius of 50 kms (about 30 miles):

Arrens, Barèges, Gavarnie-Les-Espécières, Le Hautacam, Luz-Ardiden, La Mongie, Piau-Engaly, Saint-Lary.

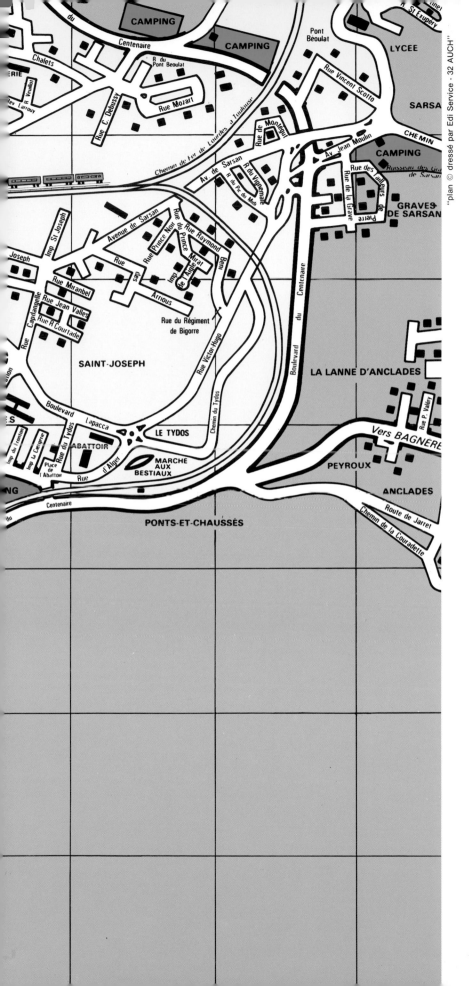

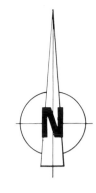

1 - The Basilica
2 - The Grotto of the Apparitions
3 - The Underground Basilica
4 - The Castle
5 - The Parish Church
6 - The Post Office and Telephones
7 - The Birthplace of Bernadette
8 - The Railway Station
9 - The Congress Hall
10 - The Town Hall
11 - The Market
12 - The Bus Station
13 - The Cemetery
14 - The Pic du Jer funicular railway
15 - The Béout cable-car
16 - Car Park
17 - Stations of the Cross
18 - War memorial
19 - The open-air swimming-pool
20 - The festival Hall, the indoor swimming-pool
21 - The Pic du Jer
22 - The Béout
23 - The Tourist Office
24 - The Cachot
25 - The City of the Poor
26 - The Boly Mill
27 - Petit Lourdes Museum
28 - The Wax works
29 - The Saint Bernadette Church

INDEX

ANDRÉ DOUCET ET FILS PUBLICATION
6, Place Peyramale - Tél. 05.62.94.27.08
65100 LOURDES
Photos
André Doucet Publication

Printed in Italy by Litovald